D0929479

To:

_____

From:

_____

Look Who's A Grandmother

By Dolli Tingle
Illustrated by Mary O'Keefe Young

A keepsake, a treasure,
an heirloom to be.
This book is all about my new
grandchild and me.

I knew the day
I saw this child
That here was genius
And I smiled,
For from a family
So select,
It's only what
One would expect.

My Beautiful Grandchild

place photo here

First Time I Saw Baby

Where _**I.C.U.** Sparrow Hospital_

When _____

Baby was _a few min._ old

My thoughts _____

_____

_____

_____

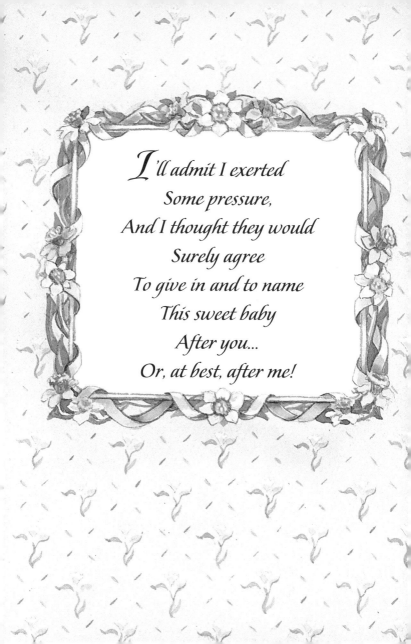

I'll admit I exerted
Some pressure,
And I thought they would
Surely agree
To give in and to name
This sweet baby
After you...
Or, at best, after me!

Baby Was Named

Reasons Why

Baby's Vital Statistics

Born on _____

At _____ o'clock ___ M

Place _____

Weight _____ Height _____

Color of eyes _____ Hair _____

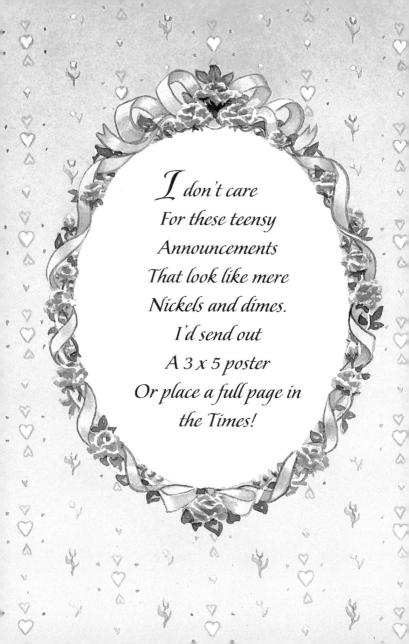

I don't care
For these teensy
Announcements
That look like mere
Nickels and dimes.
I'd send out
A 3 x 5 poster
Or place a full page in
the Times!

Announcement

*place announcement
here*

Newspapers

*place newspaper
announcement
here*

*W*ho does the baby
Resemble?
It's really quite easy to see.
Study both Mom's and
Dad's faces
Then look at the baby
And me!

Mom and Dad

Mom's name _____

Dad's name _____

Address _____

_____

place photo of
family
here

 # Brothers and Sisters

_____

_____

Baby resembles _____

_____

Sister

Mom

Baby

Grandmother/Grandfather

Great-grandmother/Great-grandfather

Great-grandmother/Great-grandfather

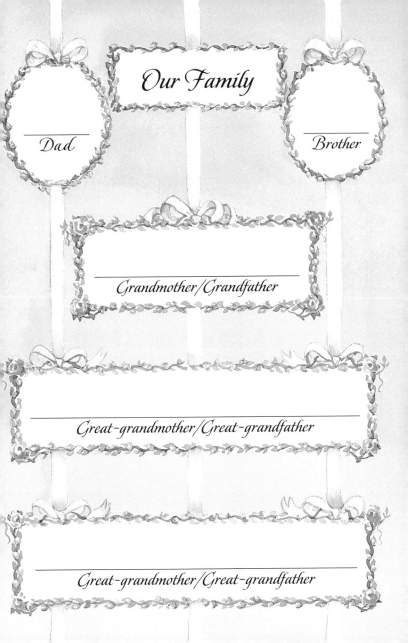

Our Family

Dad

Brother

Grandmother/Grandfather

Great-grandmother/Great-grandfather

Great-grandmother/Great-grandfather

Baby,
You're a new branch
Of our family tree
Here's your parents'
And grandparents'
History.

Who Was Born
When and Where

	Name	Date	Place
Mom			
Grandmother			
Great-grandmother			
Great-grandfather			
Grandfather			
Great-grandmother			
Great-grandfather			

Dad			
Grandmother			
Great-grandmother			
Great-grandfather			
Grandfather			
Great-grandmother			
Great-grandfather			

*Our baby came to
Visit me.
We laughed and played
'Til half past three.
Then (here's a secret
You can keep)
The two of us
Fell fast asleep.*

Baby's First Visit to Me

When _____

Where_____

What we did _____

_____

_____

_____

My Thoughts

_____

_____

_____

_____

_____

_____

We go to the park
For a ride on the swings.
We see flowers and squirrels
And all sorts of new things.
We watch little dogs
And the children at play,
And then we go home
For we've had a big day.

Outings With Baby

When _____

Where _____

_____

What we did _____

_____

_____

More Outings With Baby

When _____

Where _____

_____

What we did _____

_____

_____

You have a new Grandchild!
I just heard the news.
How perfectly madly divine!
I'll give you five minutes
To brag about yours
If you'll then let me
Talk about mine!

Our Baby is So Smart

I'll Always Remember

Guess what has
Happened
While you've been away.
Our very first tooth
Just popped out
Today!

Baby's First Smile

Baby's First Tooth

Baby Sits Up

I know you think
It's all just talk.
But in two days
This kid could walk!

Baby's First Steps

Baby's First Word

Baby Calls Grandmother

I remembered
You said
Don't get baby
Too much.
So there's no need
To scold me or fret.
I only picked up
A few wee little things
That old Santa, poor dear,
Might forget.

Baby's First Holidays

When _____

Where _____

_____

How we celebrated _____

_____

_____

_____

_____

*place
Baby's holiday photo
here*

*O*ne year old
And time to bake
A very special
Birthday cake.
Blow out the candles.
You'll get your wish.
Then eat some ice cream.
How delish!

Baby's First Birthday

When _____

Where _____

How we celebrated _____

_____

_____

My Letter to Baby

Dear _____

_____

_____

_____

_____

_____

_____

_____

_____

First Birthday Photo

place photo here

Other Photos

place photos here

*M*y grandchild, this keepsake
Is for you to treasure
And remember
As you grow
I'll love you forever.

Photo of Grandmother
and Baby

place photo here